EPIC

EPIC BOOKS are no ordinary books. They burst with intense action, high-speed heroics, and shadows of the unknown. Are you ready for an Epic adventure?

This edition first published in 2026 by Bellwether Media, Inc.

No part of this publication may be reproduced in whole or in part without written permission of the publisher. For information regarding permission, write to Bellwether Media, Inc., Attention: Permissions Department, 3500 American Blvd W, Suite 150, Bloomington, MN 55431.

Library of Congress Cataloging-in-Publication Data

LC record for Regeneration available at: https://lccn.loc.gov/2025021817

Text copyright © 2026 by Bellwether Media, Inc. EPIC and associated logos are trademarks and/or registered trademarks of Bellwether Media, Inc. Bellwether Media is a division of FlutterBee Education Group.

Editor: Rachael Barnes   Designer: Gabriel Hilger

Printed in the United States of America, North Mankato, MN.

TABLE OF CONTENTS

NO TAIL LEFT BEHIND 4
SHEDDING ANTLERS 6
SLOW GROWING STAR 10
HEALED HEARTS 14
ALL NEW TISSUE 18
GLOSSARY 22
TO LEARN MORE 23
INDEX 24

NO TAIL LEFT BEHIND

This lizard lost its tail in a fight. Luckily, the tail will grow back! Regeneration is a **rare** superpower. It means an animal can regrow a body part.

SHEDDING ANTLERS

A GREAT WEIGHT
A pair of moose antlers can weigh up to 80 pounds (36 kilograms)!

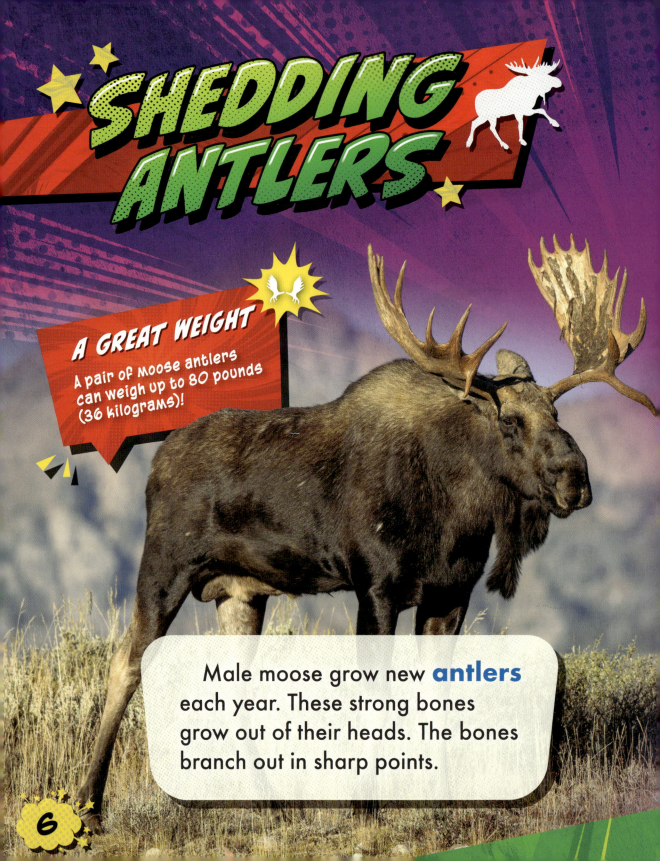

Male moose grow new **antlers** each year. These strong bones grow out of their heads. The bones branch out in sharp points.

Each year, their antlers grow bigger. They have more points than last year.

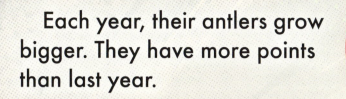

MOOSE

CLASS: MAMMAL

LIFE SPAN: UP TO 20 YEARS

STATUS IN THE WILD

| LEAST CONCERN | NEAR THREATENED | VULNERABLE | ENDANGERED | CRITICALLY ENDANGERED | EXTINCT IN THE WILD | EXTINCT |

RANGE

MATE

FIGHTING

Male moose use their antlers to get a **mate**. They use them to fight other males, too.

In the winter, moose **shed** their antlers. The bones regrow in the spring.

SLOW GROWING STAR

CENTER DISK

ARM

Sea stars dot the ocean floor. They are also called starfish.

Sea stars have a center disk. Five or more arms grow out from it. These arms help sea stars move and crawl.

SUNFLOWER SEA STAR

CLASS: INVERTEBRATE

LIFE SPAN: UP TO 65 YEARS

STATUS IN THE WILD

| LEAST CONCERN | NEAR THREATENED | VULNERABLE | ENDANGERED | CRITICALLY ENDANGERED | EXTINCT IN THE WILD | EXTINCT |

RANGE

But sea stars can heal their **injuries**. They can regrow most of their body within one year!

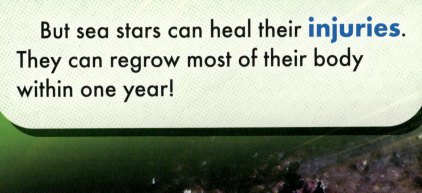

SEA STAR OR STARFISH?

Sea stars are not fish! Fish have backbones. Sea stars are related to other sea creatures with spiny skin.

HEALED HEARTS

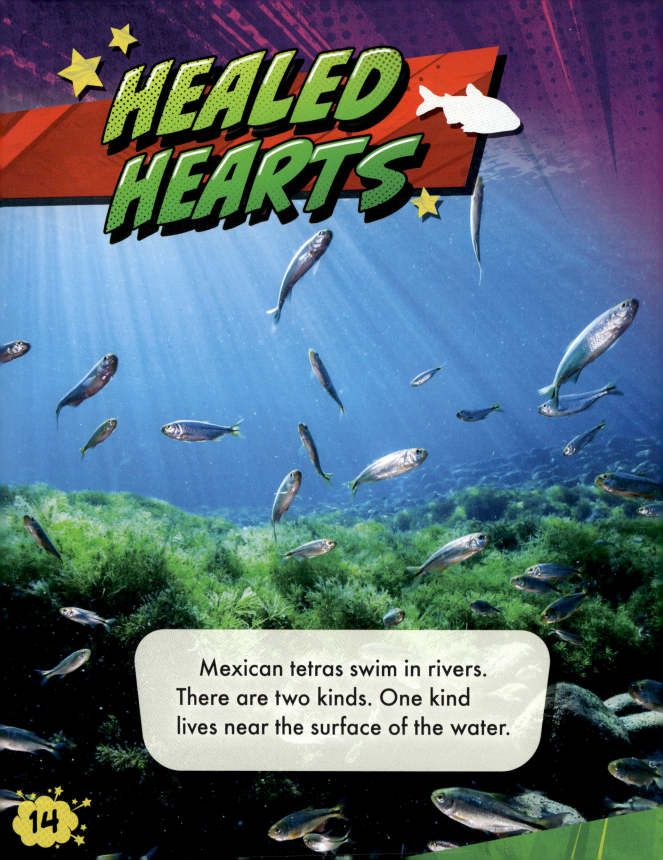

Mexican tetras swim in rivers. There are two kinds. One kind lives near the surface of the water.

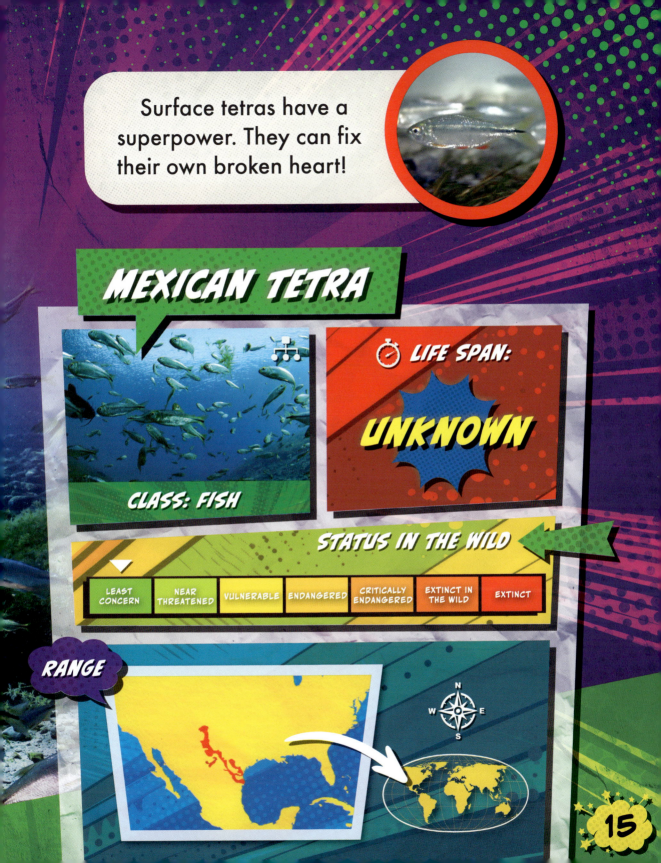

When a heart is damaged, **scars** usually form. But scars stop a heart from working well.

Surface tetras can regenerate their heart **tissue**. They can fully heal their heart!

ALL NEW TISSUE

Axolotls are **amphibians**. But unlike most amphibians, they spend their lives entirely underwater.

Axolotls might get hurt or lose a leg in an attack. But they can regrow many body parts!

AXOLOTL

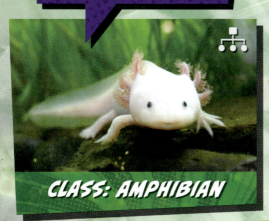

CLASS: AMPHIBIAN

LIFE SPAN:

10 TO 15 YEARS

STATUS IN THE WILD

| LEAST CONCERN | NEAR THREATENED | VULNERABLE | ENDANGERED | CRITICALLY ENDANGERED | EXTINCT IN THE WILD | EXTINCT |

RANGE

19

Axolotls can replace tissue for lost limbs or **organs**. This happens in only a few weeks!

LEG REGROWTH IN ACTION!

1. 2. 3. 4. 5.

HURT

HEALED

Animals that regrow body parts often live longer. New body parts can give them new life.

A RARE FIND
Axolotls are only found in a few lakes in Mexico.

GLOSSARY

amphibians—animals that can live on land and in water

antlers—branched bones on the heads of some animals; antlers look like horns.

injuries—pains or damages to the body

mate—one of a pair of adult animals that produce offpsring

organs—parts of the body that have a certain purpose; the skin, heart, and lungs are organs.

rare—not common

scars—marks that are left showing where something has been hurt or damaged

shed—to lose something on the body such as fur or skin

tissue—the material that forms the parts in a plant or animal

TO LEARN MORE

AT THE LIBRARY

Bassier, Emma. *Starfish*. Minneapolis, Minn.: Pop!, 2020.

Grack, Rachel. *Axolotls*. Minneapolis, Minn.: Bellwether Media, 2023.

McClure, Leigh. *Animal Adaptations*. Buffalo, N.Y.: Cavendish Square Publishing, 2025.

ON THE WEB

Factsurfer.com gives you a safe, fun way to find more information.

1. Go to www.factsurfer.com.

2. Enter "regeneration" into the search box and click 🔍.

3. Select your book cover to see a list of related content.

INDEX

amphibians, 18
antler regrowth in action, 9
antlers, 6, 7, 8, 9
arms, 10, 11, 12
attack, 12, 19
axolotls, 18, 19, 20, 21
backbones, 13
center disk, 10, 11
escape, 12
fight, 4, 8
heads, 6
heal, 13, 17
heart, 15, 16, 17
lakes, 21
leg, 19
leg regrowth in action, 20
limbs, 20
lizard, 4
mate, 8

Mexican tetras, 14, 15, 16, 17
Mexico, 21
moose, 6, 7, 8, 9
name, 10
ocean floor, 10
organs, 20
range, 7, 11, 15, 19
rivers, 14
scars, 16
sea stars, 10, 11, 12, 13
shed, 9, 12
size, 6, 7
spring, 9
sunflower sea star, 11
tail, 4
tissue, 17, 20
winter, 9

The images in this book are reproduced through the courtesy of: Narek87, front cover; David, p. 3; Robert HENNO/ Alamy Stock Photo, p. 4; saratm, p. 5; Tom Tietz, pp. 6, 7 (class: mammal); Danita Delimont, p. 7 (inset); Kelp Grizzly Photography, p. 8 (fighting); Richard Seeley, pp. 8-9; imageBROKER.com/ Alamy Stock Photo, pp. 9 (spring), 11 (class: invertebrate); Nicole Tow, p. 9 (summer); David Osborn, p. 9 (fall); moose henderson, p. 9 (winter); RLS Photo, p. 10; Reimar, p. 11 (inset); valda butterworth, pp. 12, 13; Stocktrek Images, Inc./ Alamy Stock Photo, pp. 14, 16; Clinton & Charles Robertson/ Wikipedia, p. 15 (inset); Amar and Isabelle Guillen - Guillen Photo LLC/ Alamy Stock Photo, p. 15 (class: fish); Vladimir Wrangel, p. 17; Andrea Izzotti, p. 18; Ива Димова, p. 19 (inset); kiko, p. 19 (class: amphibian); axolotlowner, p. 20 (hurt, healed); Andreas Gruhl, p. 21; Harry Collins, p. 23.

24